British Museum Object in Focus

The Asante Ewer

Lloyd de Beer
Julie Hudson
Ivor Agyeman-Duah

This publication has been made possible thanks to the generous support of Sam Fogg and Nicholas and Jane Ferguson.

First published in the United Kingdom in 2025 by The British Museum Press

A division of The British Museum Company Ltd
The British Museum
Great Russell Street
London WC1B 3DG
britishmuseum.org/publishing

A catalogue record for this book is available from the British Library.

ISBN 9780714138015
Imp-1

Layout and typesetting by Adrian Hunt
Colour reproduction by Altaimage
Printed in the UK by Park

EU Authorised Representative:
Success Courier SL, Calle Rio Tormes Num. 1, Planta 1, Derecha, Oficina 3, Fuenlabrada, Madrid, 28947, Spain.
eu-rsp@vatai.com

Further information about the British Museum and its collection can be found at britishmuseum.org.

Front cover: The Asante Ewer, *c.* 1340–1405. British Museum, 1896,0727.1.

Human remains in the British Museum
The study of human remains provides a unique insight into the lives of people from the past. The British Museum is committed to curating human remains with care, respect and dignity. Find out more about our principles governing the holding, display, care and study of human remains on the Museum website: britishmuseum.org/humanremains.

The papers used in this book are natural, renewable and recyclable and the manufacturing processes are expected to conform to the regulations of the country of origin.

Contents

Historical note

The Republic of Ghana is located on the West African coast, with its landlocked borders orientated towards the Sahel, Sudan and the Sahara desert. Its southern and central regions are home to several ethnic groups known collectively as the Akan, with shared belief systems, language and cultural traditions. Archaeological evidence and oral histories indicate that these communities migrated to their current locations over several centuries. Prominent among them are the Asante people, with political, cultural and royal power centred on the city of Kumasi.

According to Asante tradition, around 1700 a local ruler called Osei Tutu, along with the legendary priest Anokye, united a group of Akan chiefdoms around Kumasi to form the Asante confederacy. This new kingdom was legitimised by a unique stool (the Golden Stool) that descended from the sky and which symbolised and embodied the soul of the entire nation and continues to play a pivotal cultural role today.

Asante's wealth was based on its control of the Akan gold fields, an industry supported by a huge, enslaved workforce. Gold dominated the economy, functioning as a currency and as a trading commodity. The kingdom's role in the internal African trade in gold reinforced its position as a powerful state with links to major centres on the historical trans-Saharan networks and, by extension, to North Africa, the Mediterranean, the Middle East and Europe.

As for the Atlantic trade, by the late 1400s Europeans had arrived on the West African (Guinea) coast. The significant gold resources in the region prompted them to name it the 'Gold Coast', its internal territory encompassing much of modern Ghana. In 1482 the Portuguese built Elmina Castle as their base to control the lucrative trade in gold and ivory. However, under the Dutch in the mid-1600s, Elmina was primarily used as a prison for enslaved people awaiting their enforced transport to Brazil and the Caribbean. Increasingly, the Gold Coast became the focus of competing European interests, and this is reflected in the huge proliferation of forts occupied at various times by Dutch, Danish, British, German, Spanish and Swedish traders along its shoreline. Ultimately, British interests prevailed. In 1821 the British government seized territory along the coastline and declared the Gold Coast a Crown colony, establishing its capital at Cape Coast and installing a succession of governors. This threatened Asante dominance in the region, which reached the peak of its power under Asantehene Osei Bonsu (1779–1824), king of the Asante people.

By the late 1800s Britain was expanding its control beyond the Gold Coast colony, particularly in the face of pressure from France and Germany, whose governments were also seeking to enlarge their respective African colonies. Britain's policy of conquest and political suppression led to a series of wars against the Asante Kingdom – known as the Anglo-Asante wars – that sought to dismantle the power and authority of Asante and to establish British control and domination in the region. The most violent and widely publicised of these conflicts, called the Third Anglo-Asante War (1873–4), saw the British army invade Kumasi and destroy part of the city. Asantehene Kofi Karikari (*c.* 1837–*c.* 1884) was deposed and obliged to pay an indemnity to cover the costs of the British military expedition. In 1895–6 the British army attacked again and when the Asantehene Prempeh I (1870–1931) refused to surrender his sovereignty, he was also deposed and forced to sign a treaty of protection. Along with the Asantehemaa (Queen Mother) Yaa Akyaa (*c.* 1847–1917) and a large contingent of Asante chiefs, he was eventually sent into exile in the Seychelles.

In 1900, in a decisive move, the Asante people, led by the Queen Mother of Ejisu, Yaa Asantewaa (*c.* 1840–1921), rose up against the British in defence of the Golden Stool. The uprising was defeated and Yaa Asantewaa was also sent into exile in the Seychelles. This marked the end of an independent Asante kingdom. Colonial rule was established when the Asante territories were incorporated into Britain's Gold Coast colony on 1 January 1902.

Prempeh I was eventually allowed to return from exile in 1924, initially designated by the British as a private citizen and then as Kumasihene (ruler of Kumasi). The Asante territories were partially restored by the British under his successor, who was installed as Asantehene Prempeh II in 1935. On 6 March 1957 the former British colony of the Gold Coast became the independent nation-state, Ghana.

Introduction

A black-and-white photograph presents an open-air courtyard, enclosed on two sides by impressive timber buildings with plastered walls, raised floors, columned verandas and steep thatched roofs (fig. 1). The upper levels are painted with white clay, while the lower sections, with step entrances, have dark polished surfaces decorated with striking low-relief designs in swirling patterns. Between the columns, mostly hidden in shadows, are several figures: five African men dressed in wraparound cloths, most of whom face the photographer, and a European man in military clothing, shown with his upper body in shadow and carrying a walking stick, positioned casually with one leg crossed over the other, his left hand in his pocket. This image, one of a sequence, is now located in the National Archives, Kew, but originally came from the collection of the British Colonial Office, the government body responsible for the oversight of Britain's sprawling empire. The scene was captured by Accra-born

photographer Frederick Grant in 1884, and the cover of the volume is embossed with the words 'Gold Coast, Views in Kumasi: Kwaka Dua and his Court'. This title locates the image in West Africa, in what is modern-day Ghana, at the heart of the Asante Kingdom in its capital of Kumasi.

At the centre of the photograph are two spindly trees with forked branches, growing from the buttress of a much older exposed root system, which rises out of the ground like a sinuous mound. Immediately to the right of the trees, embedded in the root mound itself, are two metal jugs, made not in Africa but in Europe, in the late 1300s or 1400s. These objects are the subject of this book, which questions when and how the jugs arrived in West Africa. It investigates their shifting status, use and significance, and then explores the context for their removal from the courtyard and subsequent acquisition and redisplay in late 1800s Britain. By unravelling their 'biographies' as far as possible, the objects are traced from late medieval Europe to Africa, illustrating the extent of global pre-colonial connections and providing insights into their African life stories. However, the more recent history of the metal vessels foregrounds tense Anglo-Asante relationships brought about by British policies of control and domination in the region leading to violent clashes. These two jugs offer a fascinating lens through which to explore different but intersecting histories and, despite their place of origin being Europe, they also provide an opportunity to reflect on the complex and often paradoxical status of African objects in western European museums today.

1 View of a royal courtyard in Kumasi, 1884. Photograph by Frederick Grant. The National Archives, TNA CO 1069/31 (17).

TRYIDOWTE
BEST IN EVERY
HE SCHALL NOT

1 What is the Asante Ewer?

The largest jug appearing in Frederick Grant's photograph is today cared for by the British Museum (fig. 2). It is popularly known as the Asante Ewer, the term 'ewer' being a medieval name for a jug, derived from the Old French word 'ewe' for water. In addition to its intriguing West African provenance, the jug is a remarkable object for being the largest surviving vessel in bronze (an alloy of copper and tin) made in medieval England. Pear-shaped, with an elongated neck and a broad, rounded belly, it displays a sharp, deep triangular spout and a thick ridged handle terminating in a four-petalled openwork disc. Still retaining its original heptagonal (seven-sided) fluted lid, the ewer measures an impressive 62 centimetres in height (43 centimetres tall without the lid). When empty, the jug weighs nearly 19 kilograms and has the capacity to carry almost 19 litres of liquid – which would bring the overall weight to 38 kilograms. Given its massive overall size and heft, when full it must have required careful handling to pour liquids without disaster and possibly needed more than one person to avoid spillage.

Much smaller hand-held jugs with directional spouts – often called lavers (from the Old French 'laveor', 'washing') – were used for cleaning hands before or after a meal. The size of the Asante Ewer suggests that it served another function, but its original use or role remains uncertain. If used for serving wine, its contents must have been very carefully poured out from a stationary stand or perhaps ladled into smaller jugs or separate cups. There is little doubt, however, that this was an object made to be seen. Display was an integral part of medieval feasting, where the status of the host was demonstrated through the ostentatious use of metal objects, with gold and silver being the most esteemed signifiers of wealth and luxury. While not made from one of those precious metals, the scale, weight and decoration of the Asante Ewer would have signalled the wealth of its owner and identified it as a high-status item to be displayed as part of the household wares on grand occasions. At the most sumptuous dinners, a dresser or sideboard was set

2 The Asante Ewer, c. 1340–1405. England. Leaded bronze. H. 62 cm. British Museum, 1896,0727.1.

3 Philippe Camus, *Histoire d'Olivier de Castille et d'Artus d'Algarbe*, c. 1460. Flanders, Bruges. Ink on parchment. H. 14 cm, W. 14.5 cm. Bibliothèque nationale de France, Paris, Français 12574, f. 181v.

A feasting scene with large metalwork ewers shown standing on the floor (lower right).

with smaller expensive items, whereas larger vessels stood on the floor (fig. 3).

Another suggestion, from art historians Julian Luxford and Philippe Cordez, is that the jug might have functioned as a standard of measurement, perhaps in the trading of wine.[1] From the 1300s onwards, standard measurements were distributed throughout England to ensure fair trade. The earliest surviving vessels date to the late 1400s, such as an inscribed bronze jug from the reign of Henry VII made for measuring out a medieval gallon (about 4 litres) of wine, now in the collection of the Science Museum, London (acc. no. 1931-1013). Tantalisingly, a print by the engraver and antiquary George Vertue from the 1700s records 'The Standard of Weights and Measures in the Exchequer'. This is a copy he made of an illuminated parchment pasted onto an oak board in the treasury of the king's exchequer (finance office) at Westminster. The document makes reference to, and includes images of, metal jugs of various sizes that were used to regulate the trading of wine in England.

While at first glance the monochrome bronze jug might seem plain, its artistic, technical and literary merits come to the fore upon closer attention. Its outer body is selectively decorated, displaying two textual inscriptions and a variety of embossed signs comprising heraldry and animal images. Wrapped around the vessel's belly, notably in English rather than French or Latin, is the inscription (reading from the bottom line upwards):

> *+ HE THAT WYL NOT SPARE WHAN HE MAY HE SCHAL NOT SPEND WHAN HE WOLD*
> *DEME THE BEST IN EVERY DOWT TIL THE TROWTHE BE TRYID OWTE*

These two epigrams read like proverbs, the first encouraging the reader to save wisely ('spare whan he may') so that 'he' can spend when needed, the equivalent of saving your money for a rainy day. If the first sentence is about frugality, then the second implores good judgement, telling those in front of the jug to act justly until the truth can be proven ('til the trowthe be tryid owte'). Why a metal jug would direct those in its vicinity towards financial and judicial prudence is made all the more fascinating when the entire decorative scheme is considered.

Beneath the spout, shown between two supporting lions, is a crowned version of the English royal coat of arms (fig. 4), a quartered shield made up of the fleurs-de-lys of France and the leopards or lions of England. Other images on the jug are drawn from the world of medieval heraldry and bolster the armorial display. A series of six beaded roundels showing eagles or falcons, their wings partially spread out and heads held up proudly, are equally distributed either side of the

4 Detail of the English royal coat of arms on the Asante Ewer, showing a quartered shield with the fleurs-de-lys of France and the leopards or lions of England.

5 **Detail of eagles or falcons on the Asante Ewer.**

vessel's neck (fig. 5). Two are located near the spout, with the other four positioned either side of the handle. The lid is divided into seven parts, each facet containing an image of a standing lion, under which lies a resting stag with long antlers (fig. 6).

The resting stag, frequently identified as the White Hart, has led some scholars to suggest the jug might have been made for King Richard II of England (1367–1400). Richard adopted the White Hart as his personal emblem, possibly a visual play on his name *Rich-hart*, and the animal appears in various locations connected with his royal patronage, for instance, as a wall painting in Westminster Abbey, and as an incised design on his virtuoso gilded brass effigy, also at Westminster. The best-known depictions of the White Hart, however, are those on the Wilton Diptych, a two-part panel painting commissioned by Richard. On the inside, the diptych shows Richard kneeling in devotion, with saints Edmund, Edward the Confessor and John the Baptist standing to his side (fig. 7). Here, the White Hart decorates the sumptuous cloth brocade of his gold and burnt orange cloak, but it is

6 Detail of the lid of the Asante Ewer, showing lions (above) and resting stags (below).

also worn by Richard and the angels surrounding the Virgin and Child as a precious white ronde-bosse (in the round) enamel brooch. On the outside of the painting, the White Hart appears as a living creature shown lying in a verdant field (fig. 8). In each of these instances the Hart wears a crown and a chain around its neck.

On the lid of the ewer, the surface quality of the original casting is heavily abraded, making it difficult to determine whether the resting stags wore a crown and chain. While the comparisons remain compelling for a royal connection, and despite a clear scholarly desire to assign a patron to the jug, there is no absolute evidence tying the Asante Ewer to Richard's household. As historian of heraldry Michael Siddons has pointed out, the Hart was in use as a royal symbol by Edward III (1312–1377), Richard's grandfather, prior to his adoption of it.[2] Without further evidence to tie the vessel conclusively to Richard, some caution must be exercised in associating it with him exclusively. Nevertheless, the likely cost of production, as well as its size, decoration and

7 The Wilton Diptych, 1390–5. England or France (?). Egg tempera on wood. H. 53 cm, W. 37 cm. The National Gallery, London, NG4451.

8 Reverse of the Wilton Diptych, showing the White Hart (bottom right).

potential function – to serve wine at a grand feast – all mark the object out as a status symbol par excellence, affordable only to the wealthy elite, and comfortably at home in the royal household or that of a person distinguished enough to display the arms and badges of royalty. It is therefore relatively safe to assume that the ewer's text spoke to individuals of exactly these social strata, encouraging them towards virtuous behaviour: to not spend their money unwisely (or, perhaps, to pour wine excessively) and to judge others justly. If the jug had been owned by an English king, then this is sage advice indeed as the monarch was deemed to be the ultimate earthly authority and the model of faultless behaviour. Alternatively, if the jug was used as a standard for measurement in the trading of wine, then its text and decoration also support this potential function. The heraldry and badges reveal the king's role in overseeing fair trade, and the text, which speaks to good judgement and prudence, might have served as a subtle warning to traders looking to deceive.

Given the lack of certainty about whom exactly the jug may have been made for and when, accurately dating its production is a challenge. The royal arms beneath the spout help to provide a broad date range as a starting point for its production, its earliest use being around 1340, when King Edward III first quartered the French and English shields, to around 1405, when King Henry IV (1367–1413) reduced the number of fleurs-de-lys to three. Some scholars have devised dating trajectories based on the style of inscriptions, for instance those on memorial brasses made for individuals whose life and death dates can be easily ascertained.[3] The text on the Asante Ewer is in a style called Lombardic which, roughly speaking, was eventually replaced in the second half of the 1300s by another style of script, called Black Letter. Although the use of Lombardic script on the Asante Ewer suggests a date well before 1400, a broad date range for its production, as signified by the royal heraldry, of between 1340 and 1405, is perhaps the safest option.

While the Asante Ewer is certainly the largest known English medieval bronze vessel, two remarkably similar though somewhat smaller jugs survive, both of which have seemingly remained in England since their manufacture

9 The Wenlock Jug (left), the Robinson Jug (middle) and the Asante Ewer (right).

(fig. 9). These are known as the Robinson and Wenlock jugs, which, along with the Asante Ewer, have different provenance histories indicating that they were not part of a group made for, or owned by, the same person. As will be shown, however, similarities in material, style and production technique suggest that all three jugs were produced in the same foundry, one which very likely also produced bells. The Robinson Jug (fig. 10) is named after its former owner, the artist and collector John Charles Robinson (d. 1913), who sold it to the Victoria and Albert Museum (then the South Kensington Museum) in 1879. According to records associated with the acquisition, it was originally found in an old manor house in Norfolk, although exactly where this house was located remains unknown. At 38.5 centimetres tall, and lacking its lid, the jug is almost 5 centimetres smaller than the British Museum's vessel. Like the Asante Ewer, two English epigrams are wrapped around its belly:

> *+ GODDIS GRACE BE IN THIS PLACE AMEN.*
> *+ STOND VTTIR FROM THE FYRE AND LAT ON IVST COME NERE*

The Wenlock Jug (fig. 11) came to the attention of scholars in 2005 when it was auctioned by Sotheby's on behalf of Alexander Fermor-Hesketh, 3rd Baron Hesketh, at Easton Neston House in Northamptonshire, England, as part of a three-day sale of the house contents. Following an export ban, it was bought by The Culture Trust, Luton, Bedfordshire, England. At 31 centimetres high, this vessel is the smallest of the three and, like the Robinson Jug, is lacking its lid. Its size and the brevity of its textual inscription – simply stating 'MY LORD WENLOK' – might suggest it is the least interesting example in the group. However, the

10 The Robinson Jug, *c.* 1340–1405. England. Leaded bronze. H. 38.5 cm. Victoria and Albert Museum, London, A 217-1879.

11 The Wenlock Jug, *c.* 1340–1405. England. Leaded bronze. H. 31 cm. Luton Museums Service, 2006/28.

a

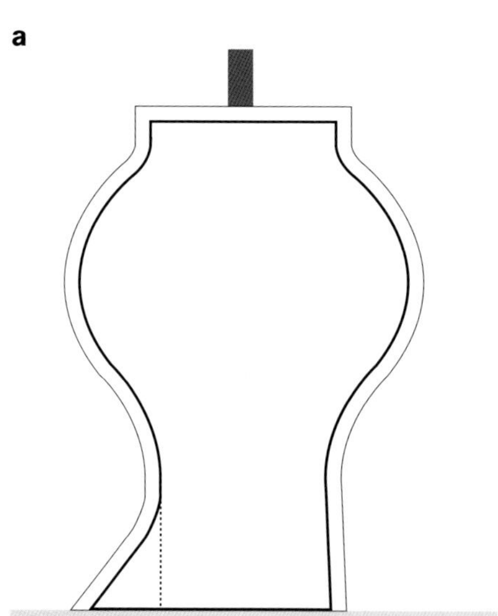

b

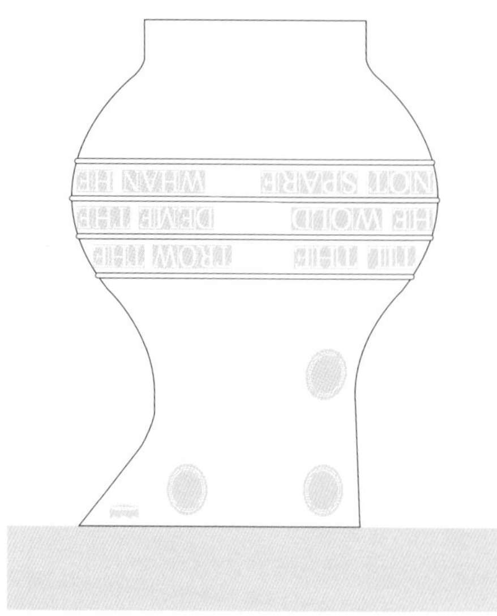

c

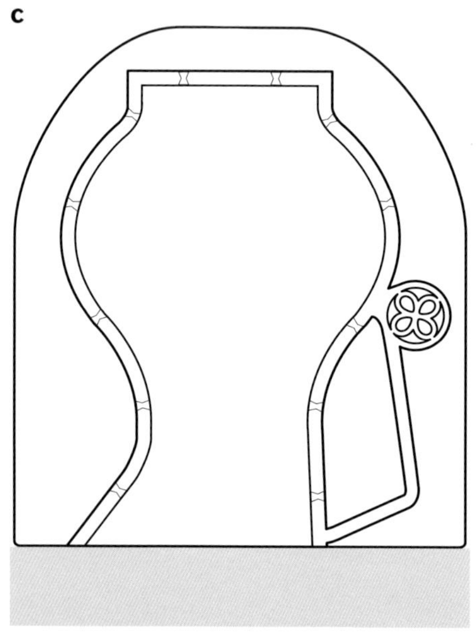

d

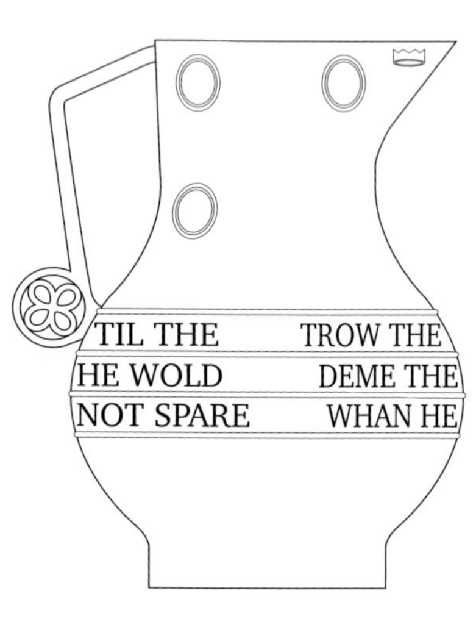

12 Drawing proposing the sequence of processes for making the Asante Ewer.

naming of a person provides clear documentary evidence for an original owner, not seen on the others. Exactly who 'Wenlok' was remains a mystery. The jug has previously been linked to a branch of the Wenlock family that ultimately settled in Luton (hence the local interest in its acquisition) and particularly that of William Wenlock (d. 1391), or his great-nephew John Wenlock (d. 1471) who was made the first Lord Wenlock by Edward IV in 1461. But the mid-1400s date of John's ennoblement is somewhat later than the generally assumed period of production for the jug and its counterparts (*c.* 1340–1405) and, furthermore, the Wenlocks of Bedfordshire were just one branch of a large family line, so the ewer's original owner remains to be discovered.

Neither the Robinson nor the Wenlock jug displays an image of the White Hart but both have lost their lids, which is where the animal is located on the Asante Ewer, so it is uncertain whether motifs like the White Hart were originally present. The jugs, nevertheless, share much in common, from crowns to royal heraldry to the position and format of their textual inscriptions, and there is further evidence to connect them beyond doubt. Scientific study and close analysis of the jugs by scientist Susan La Niece and art historian Marian Campbell have shown that these vessels share a similar bronze composition (with high lead content) and were cast by the same process in a two-part cope mould (fig. 12).[4] The pronounced seams or 'flashlines' running along the sides and across the base of all three jugs show where the moulds were joined during firing.

To achieve the final product, a lengthy and complex construction and firing process took place, which remains difficult to explain with absolute certainty. What follows is conjectural. First, a central core, probably made up of a mixture of brick or rubble, was built around a spindle on a raised base. Soft clay was slathered around the core, then shaped using a template into the form of an upside-down ewer without a spout. Another more friable (crumbly) clay-like material was then applied to the core to create a 'false jug'; this layer would be destroyed prior to casting. Once complete the spout was added (fig. 12a). Then the ewer's design was arranged, probably applied to a wax overlay using moulds or stamps (the text, crowns and royal heraldry on all three vessels were demonstrably made from the same matrices, all sharing the exact same measurements, for instance) (fig. 12b). At this point the entire 'false jug' was probably coated in a material (ash) to prevent the mould from sticking when the next layer of clay was applied. The ensemble was then encased in wet clay to create the outer mould, which was left to dry, or it may have been fired. Next, the outer mould was cut into two parts vertically to separate it from the core beneath and the friable material was chiselled away to create a cavity. Bronze spacers were placed between the mould and core to maintain separation, and then the two-part mould was placed back over the core. It was possibly at this point, prior to pouring, that the handle was added, potentially as a separate mould inserted into a cut-out section of the larger mould (fig. 12c). The bronze was poured into the mould and, after being left to cool, the mould was broken with a hammer and any excess clay was chipped away. Flashlines or imperfections were chased back with a chisel and other tools to render the surface flush. Following this the jug was cleaned and polished (fig. 12d).

This suggested process of production is consistent with established methods for making bells in medieval England and much of Europe, although bells were usually made in a single mould. In the case of the ewers, the two-part mould was selected because of the jugs' spouts and handles: it would have been impossible to lift a single mould from the 'false jug' without breaking it. The suggestion that these ewers were produced in a bell-foundry was first made in the late 1800s by Charles Hercules Read, the British Museum curator responsible for acquiring the Asante Ewer. In the first publication featuring it, he wrote: 'This noble jug was no doubt the work of one of the bellfounders of the time, for the style of the letters and the method of using them is in exact accordance with those found on the old English church bells.'[5] That English bell-founders also made smaller domestic wares, such as tripod-ewers, mortars and other types of jug, is well established. A Thomas Potter, for instance, is documented working in Norwich around the same time of the ewer's production, that is in the mid-1300s,

13 Seal matrix of Sandre de Gloucester, 1200–1300. England. Bronze. H. 3.2 cm, W. 2 cm. British Museum, 1889,0507.33.

14 Maker's mark on the Wenlock Jug (see fig. 11).

and he used an image of a three-legged metal pot as the hallmark on his bells. Other bell-founders did the same. John Langhorne used a shield with three tripod lavers for his trademark and John de Copgrave of York's mark was a shield with a bell, a mortar and a pot. At the centre of his personal seal matrix Sandre de Gloucester, a late 1200s bell-founder, combined an inscribed tripod jug and a small bell to demonstrate the main products of his workshop (fig. 13).[6] Exactly who was responsible for the Asante Ewer and the other two vessels remains a mystery. A maker's mark can be seen on the neck of the Wenlock Jug, to the left of the handle, a feature lacking on the others, but searches for the owner of this mark have been inconclusive so far (fig. 14).

How then did the Asante Ewer – most likely the product of a medieval bell-foundry, possibly displayed and used at grand feasts or as a standard for measurement – end up in the courtyard of a royal building in West Africa? And what of the other medieval jug next to it in the Colonial Office photograph? The next chapter discusses the possible routes by which the Asante Ewer might have travelled to West Africa.

North Atlantic Ocean
UNITED KINGDOM
NETHERLANDS
GERMANY
PORTUGAL
Mediterranean Sea
SYRIA
EGYPT
SAUDI ARABIA
MALI
SIERRA LEONE
GHANA
NIGERIA
Gulf of Guinea
South Atlantic Ocean
BURKINA FASO
Black Volta
White Volta
GHANA
IVORY COAST
TOGO
Nsawkaw
Atebubu
Lake Volta
Kumasi
Sefwi
Accra
Abakrampa
Elmina
Cape Coast
0
100 miles
0
100 km

2 Material values: from England to West Africa

> *The question of the antiquity of the jug is, however, a simple matter compared with its mysterious appearance among the paraphernalia of [an African] king … It would require no great straining of probability to imagine an English ship … being carried by unfavourable winds … upon the African coast of Morocco or Tripoli. From either of these points there is a regular caravan route … whence they go due south to Timbuktu [present-day Mali]. There is, however, another trade route by which I prefer to think the jug may have travelled. In the first quarter of the fifteenth century the father of African discovery, Prince Henry the Navigator, was sending expedition after expedition down the Atlantic coast of North Africa … What is more likely than that this enlightened and learned prince, the grandson of our John of Gaunt, should have included in one of his many cargoes assorted to please the eye of native potentates a selection of English goods?*
>
> — Charles Hercules Read[7]

In 1898 British Museum curator Charles Hercules Read proffered two suggestions to the Society of Antiquaries for how the Asante Ewer might have travelled to West Africa, either via the Sahara desert by a camel caravan, or as part of the cargo of a 1400s Portuguese trading ship sent down the west coast of Africa. Subsequent scholars have taken Read's comments seriously, as they should, both being entirely possible, but his ideas were nonetheless inflected with the proud unbridled nationalism of an Englishman writing at the zenith of British imperial power, when the exploration and colonisation of vast swathes of the globe was taking place, much of it in connection with the exportation of 'English goods'.

The Asante Ewer served for Read as a medieval precursor of later British dominance of worldwide trade, a picture far from accurate for the Middle Ages. In reality, England was a minor player in the complex trade networks that connected the richer and far more powerful kingdoms of medieval West Africa with those north of the Sahara, the eastern

15 Map of Ghana in the context of Africa and Europe.

Mediterranean and mainland Europe. These were not direct connections, but ones facilitated by a series of intermediaries. Access to gold mined in the Akan forest region was the impetus for much of the trans-Saharan trade. Communities engaged in this lucrative business were established on the fringes of this forest zone from at least the 1300s to facilitate the movement of gold to major centres of exchange in the Mali Empire and beyond. The rise of European, and later British, hegemony in the centuries after 1500 has obscured the historical picture, with Africa's true role in shaping medieval global trade networks downplayed. To set the record straight, this chapter seeks to explore the story of the Asante Ewer from the perspective of its African as much as its European history. The predicament here is, however, the limited information relating to the ewer's journey and the gap between its arrival in West Africa and its earliest documentation in Frederick Grant's photograph of it (see fig. 1). Can the gaps in its documented history – from its production in medieval England to the 1884 photograph in Kumasi – be filled in?

Trans-Saharan trade

To assess the validity of Charles Read's first suggestion, that the ewer might have travelled across the Sahara, it is necessary to briefly consider the evidence for the African trade in other luxury copper items of a similar date. Raymond Silverman's pioneering research into the status of imported medieval metal objects in West Africa has greatly enhanced understanding of the surviving corpus of imported copper-alloy vessels and their wider cultural contexts.[8] In 1980 Silverman undertook fieldwork in Ghana, documenting a small but significant group of Islamic copper-alloy bowls and basins, which had been made in Mamluk-controlled Egypt or Syria in the late 1300s and 1400s, the majority of which he recorded at the northern limits of the Akan forest region (fig. 15). Like the Asante Ewer, each of the six objects surveyed by Silverman is an extraordinary example of the metalworker's craft, and all six are profusely decorated and inscribed in Arabic, some even bearing the name of the ruling sultan, court official or individual who commissioned them. One of the three bowls located at Nsawkaw, for

16 Mamluk basin, *c.* 1340–60. Copper alloy. Diam. 67 cm. Photograph by Raymond Silverman in situ at Nsawkaw, Ghana, January 1980.

example (fig. 16), can be linked via its text with an official from the court of the Mamluk ruler al-Nasir Hasan (r. 1347–51 and 1354–61). In this period, unworked copper and finished copper-alloy objects were highly prized as imports to West Africa through the trans-Saharan trade. The copper-alloy composition of these vessels, almost unknown in the Akan region prior to the arrival of these items, elevated their status and they became – and in some cases are still regarded as – highly treasured objects. Perhaps for this reason, as well as the cultural and material value accorded to them locally, the imported vessels were preserved rather than melted down, a testament to their prestigious standing.

While each vessel surveyed by Silverman can be dated to between the mid-1300s and mid-1400s, there is little surviving evidence to confirm that any of them were taken across the Sahara in the medieval period, rather than, say, at a much later date. In 1992, however, another copper-alloy Mamluk bowl was discovered during archaeological excavations by a German-Nigerian team, this time in a grave, part of a sequence of elite burials not in Ghana but in northern Nigeria, at Durbi Takusheyi, about 1,200 kilometres away. This bowl, broad and low with a band of calligraphic text and patternwork set near the rim, interspersed with florid roundels, was potentially made in the late 1300s. Archaeological evidence suggests its association with a burial,

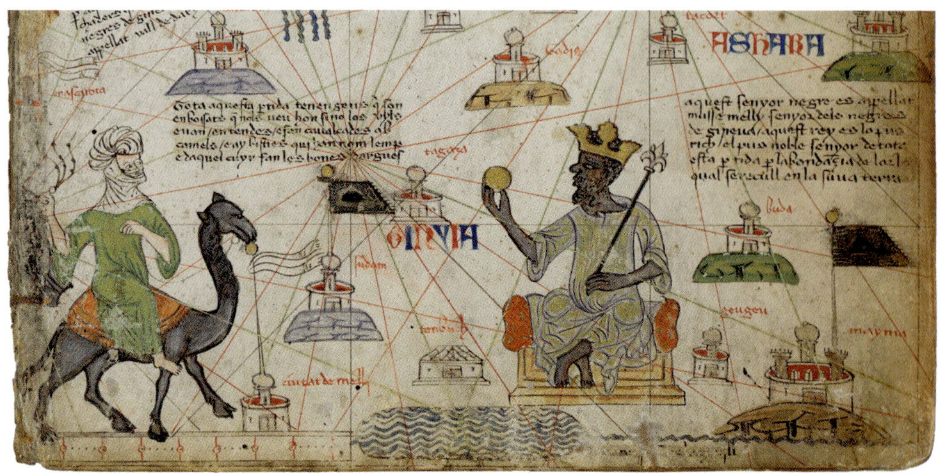

17 Abraham Cresques (?), *Atlas of Maritime Charts* (*The Catalan Atlas*), 1375. Mallorca. Ink, pen, silver and gold on parchment. H. 64.5 cm, W. 25 cm (panels). Bibliothèque nationale de France, Paris, Ms. Espagnol 30.

Mansa Musa (right), the ruler of the Mali Empire, is seated on his throne before a camel-mounted trader. He holds a gold object symbolising his extraordinary wealth.

possibly also dating to the late 1300s–1400s. The presence of gold jewellery as well as luxury goods, such as brass ingots, copper, brass and ivory bracelets, copper-alloy buckets, carnelian beads and cowrie shells, indicates its inclusion in extensive trade networks with both regional West African neighbours and long-distance communities in North Africa, the eastern Mediterranean, Europe and possibly the Middle East.

How exactly and why did these Mamluk basins travel so far from their places of production? As with the Asante Ewer, there is no documentation to answer such questions satisfactorily. Silverman has suggested that one way in which these items might have reached Ghana was as part of the luggage of West African Muslims returning from Hajj, their spiritual pilgrimage to Mecca. Wealthy individuals who could afford the journey might have been gifted or acquired luxury metalwork (for example, as a second-hand purchase in Cairo or elsewhere) that was otherwise unavailable to them at home. Although probably based to the north of Ghana in what is now modern central Mali, Mansa Musa, the ruler of the Mali Empire, who was internationally famed for his extraordinary wealth, travelled on Hajj in the 1320s, stopping in Cairo for two weeks where he was entertained by the sultan (fig. 17). Much has been written about the vast quantity

18 Left: Penny issued by Henry III, 1257. England. Gold. Weight 2.9 g. British Museum, 1915,0507.571. Right: Florin, or double-leopard, issued by Edward III, 1344. England. Gold. Weight 6.9 g. British Museum, 1915,0507.572.

of gold that Mansa Musa took with him and dispensed on his journey, but the nature of the objects he and members of his entourage might have brought back is only speculation.

Only three of the Islamic basins surveyed by Silverman are still present, in Atebubu and Nsawkaw, locations connected to the long-distance medieval trade in Akan gold across the Sahara desert. Clearly, the traders who traversed the Saharan caravan routes understood the status of luxury metalwork and sought out precious items for gifting and exchange. Copper, highly valued by West Africans of the Middle Ages on account of its rarity, was just one of a variety of luxury materials, alongside salt and textiles, that moved from north to south. Art historian Sarah Guérin has shown that, after being carried across the desert in the opposite direction, goods such as bountiful West African gold and ivory entered North Africa, Europe and Asia, even reaching England.[9] It is predominantly from West African gold that the first English gold coinage was minted after the Norman Conquest. In the mid-1200s a gold penny bearing the name of Henry III was created but quickly abandoned as viable currency, with only a few coins of this type surviving. In the 1340s a successful larger coin was established under King Edward III, grandfather to Richard II, with whom the Asante Ewer has long been associated (fig. 18).

The same can be said for the delicate gold leaves, hammer-beaten into gossamer-thin sheets from coins made from West African gold, and applied to the background,

19 Ivory triptych showing the Coronation of the Virgin, the Crucifixion and Saints Peter, Paul, Stephen and Thomas Becket, England, c. 1330–40. Ivory. H. 23.8 cm, W. 20.6 cm (open), D. 1.7 cm (open). British Museum, 1861,0416.1.

crowns and even the cloth of the infant Christ in Richard II's Wilton Diptych. In the 1330s the bishop of Exeter, John Grandisson – who enjoyed a strong relationship with mainland Europe due to his time spent in the Avignon papacy (France) – commissioned a series of ivory devotional tablets, carved in England. The enormous size of the panels suggests a West African provenance for the ivory (fig. 19). Although, when it was first produced, it would have been hard to imagine how far the Asante Ewer would eventually travel, the material presence of sub-Saharan Africa in the form of gold and ivory across Europe demonstrates the extent of pre-colonial trade.

Apart from documenting the locations of the Mamluk basins in Ghana, Silverman also demonstrated that imported metalwork from beyond the Sahara had a profound impact on indigenous metalworking traditions in the Akan region.[10] For instance, he showed that the technique, form and decoration of the imported vessels were studied and inspired the local production of a variety of West African-made metal containers called kuduo (fig. 20). None of these is known to replicate the form of the Asante Ewer, indicating its extraordinary rarity by comparison with Mamluk basins, which were in more plentiful supply. During his 1980s fieldwork Silverman also recorded contemporary oral histories associated with the vessels, elucidating their changing significance as they moved from one cultural context and function to another. In each case the item was understood not as the work of a Mamluk metalworker but either as having descended from the sky as a gift from Nyame (god) or through connection with illustrious Asante ancestors such as Kyeiwaa Nyame (goddess Kyeiwaa). In this way, the local biographies of these basins are constructed as repositories of cultural memory, the physical embodiment of Akan history, and serve to underscore and validate social structures of authority. In Asante culture, high-status regalia objects operate in much the same way: the Golden Stool, for instance, the most sacred object of the Asante people, descended from the sky into the lap of Osei Tutu, the first Asantehene (ruler of Asante people). No such oral history is known to have been recorded for the Asante Ewer.

20 Asante kuduo in the form of an imported Mamluk bowl, 1500–1600 (?). Made in Asante region. Copper alloy. H. 15 cm, Diam. 32 cm. British Museum, Af1955,05.225.

But other significant imported items documented in Kumasi or Bantama, the site of the Asante royal mausoleum, are infused with historical meaning, such as the Bobrapa Pan and Aya Kese, described more fully below. Although its story is now lost, it seems likely the Asante Ewer, as a finished imported prestige object worked in copper alloy, might also have been assimilated into Asante cultural history.

Imported items at the Asante court

The survival and photography of the Asante Ewer within the royal palace complex in Kumasi in the 1800s would alone have sufficed to make its story remarkable. However, two further medieval European vessels can also be traced to the same location. First, there is the other jug in the courtyard photograph, nestled among the tree's roots with the Asante Ewer. It too survives, now in the collection of the Prince of Wales's Own Regiment of Yorkshire, England. At 51 centimetres tall, this three-legged copper-alloy vessel is of a similar size to the Asante Ewer, but is much plainer, lacking heraldic decoration as well as, crucially, any text which, if present, might have helped identify where exactly it was produced. Aside from its three legs, it is of roughly the same shape as the Asante Ewer, comprising a broad belly, a tall neck and a sharp triangular spout. Its original lid disappeared long ago and was possibly broken off in some haste: a fractured, twisted metal stub can still be found in the hinge located where the handle joins the neck.

The current lid was in place by the time it was photographed in 1884, most likely made in West Africa. Its technique of manufacture (hammering) and metal composition (brass with minor amounts of lead) is more closely aligned with other vessels produced in the Akan region (fig. 21), as confirmed by recent analysis undertaken at the British Museum by scientists Laura Perucchetti and Aude Mongiatti. Exactly when this lid was made, however, is hard to determine. The jug's location in the royal courtyard and, more significantly, the fact it was embedded between the roots of two trees indicate that it held a comparable status to that of its partner vessel, and that they possibly served a similar function. Given the Asante Ewer's lid remained intact,

21 Jug, 1400–1500, England, Germany or the Netherlands (?), copper alloy. Lid, 1700–1880, Ghana (?), brass. H. 51 cm, W. 34 cm. Prince of Wales's Own Regiment of Yorkshire Museum Charity, TR04672.

secured to its handle by means of a rope, and that a new lid was commissioned for the other vessel at some point after it arrived in Africa, it seems that these objects were still intended as containers of some sort, or could at least be closed.

A third medieval ewer – made of leaded brass (alloy of copper and zinc with high lead content) and not appearing alongside the others in the photograph – can also be traced to Kumasi, and to the same royal context as the other two (fig. 22). It was acquired by the British Museum in 1933 following the death of its owner, Sir Cecil Armitage (1869–1933). The jug arrived at the Museum along with a British-made silver lidded punch bowl, described by Armitage as from the 'Ashanti district', its mark dating it to London, 1764, although, like the ewer in York, it shows signs of West African repair and addition (fig. 23). Today, an imported silver bowl with lid, called Dwete Kuduo (silver casket), plays an important part in Asante ceremonial life and is used exclusively by the

Asantehene for prayers and to offer libations. It is likely that the Museum's silver vessel fulfilled a similar sacred function in the Asante royal court. In oral traditions, the Dwete Kuduo is linked to Asante victory in battle and it provides protection for the Asantehene as well as giving him the strength and power required to rule his people.

Armitage had served as a captain in the 1895–6 Anglo-Asante War, later being appointed private secretary to Sir Frederick Hodgson, Governor of Britain's Gold Coast colony. Armitage was in Kumasi again in 1900, with Hodgson, whose gross insensitivity in demanding to sit on the Golden Stool incited a further Asante uprising, an unsuccessful attempt to expel the British from Kumasi. Archival documents in the British Museum associated with the jug's acquisition reference the 1900 war in connection with the vessel, describing it as a

> *Mediaeval bronze jug, one of two taken by a king of ASHANTI when he conquered SEFWHI [Sefwi], and remained in Kings palace until 1896; then carried in van of Ashanti army when it attacked the fort KUMASI on 28 April 1900 to ensure victory, captured by loyal Ashanti levies [enlisted soldiers] and presented to Capt. Armitage.*[11]

Some scholars have argued that the York and Armitage jugs were, like the Asante Ewer, also produced in England. While there is no reason to doubt that the vessels are of a medieval date – broadly late 1300s to 1400s – there is little evidence to confirm definitively that they are of English manufacture. In lieu of identifying heraldry or text, dating and locating the place of production for vessels of this sort remains a challenge. The surviving corpus of such European copper-alloy vessels is small, comprising just a handful of items, and jugs such as these were produced in various locations across Europe, including the Netherlands and Germany as well as England. The fact that the three of them share a West African provenance neither proves that they were of English production nor confirms that they travelled to Africa from England as a group. As Charles Read suggested to the Society of Antiquaries, the Asante Ewer could well have made its way from Portugal originally or from another European country that developed a trading

22 Jug, 1400–1500. England, Germany, or the Netherlands (?). Leaded brass. H. 37.5 cm, W. 26 cm. British Museum, Af1933,-.2.

23 Punch bowl, 1764. England, hallmark London. Silver. H. 22.5 cm, W. 30.3 cm. British Museum, Af1933,-.3.a-b.

relationship with West Africa from the late 1400s onwards, such as Holland. Read did not, however, know about the existence of the other two vessels when he made his remarks.

Unfortunately, there is no way of corroborating Armitage's comments on his jug's provenance, or that it was in the palace until 1896 (when it was potentially removed and safely hidden because of the Anglo-Asante War), or even that it was one of two vessels taken by Asante forces after conquering Sefwi – a rival Akan state located in western Ghana. This event, one of several local wars waged by Asante during a period of expansion and consolidation in the late 1700s, aligns with a pivotal episode in the development of Asante regional hegemony. The seizure of prestigious imported European copper-alloy vessels from defeated enemies and their subsequent use as palladia (tokens to ensure victory in battle) as well as their positioning within royal or shrine contexts in Kumasi serve as compelling material evidence of their protective role. In the case of the Asante Ewer and the York jug, these vessels appear to have been cared for in a ritualistic manner, placed at the base of trees on a mound of earth within a royal courtyard, thereby distinguishing them from any objects with a potential utilitarian function. One of the trees, the younger of the two, has a white cloth tied around the centre of its trunk, an indication of its sacred status. Parallels may be drawn with the household shrine (Nyame Dua – tree of god), a familiar sight in many Asante courtyards, comprising a three-pronged tree branch supporting metal basins in which offerings are made. Similarly, most of the Mamluk basins recorded by Silverman were associated with trees and were cared for by designated custodians to ensure prosperity and protection for the entire community.

As for the other jug Armitage connected with the defeat of Sefwi, it could be a reference to the Asante Ewer or the York vessel, or potentially to a now-lost or unidentified additional ewer. The information gathered by Armitage may have formed part of a contemporaneous inherited oral history, or was tailored to suit his perceived interest. Still, the fact that much older items like the Armitage ewer – which he describes in the language of the time as a 'war fetish' – were allegedly carried into battle by the Asante serves to underscore the potential talismanic function of luxury metalwork vessels. It also supports the development of historical memories around such vessels, in particular their association with prior successful wars that might guarantee victory in future battles.

Another significant European object associated through oral traditions with an important historical Asante battle is the large hammered-brass basin currently on display at the Prempeh II Jubilee Museum, Kumasi, known locally as the Bobrapa Pan.[12] One of the narratives recounted at the museum today is that it was sent by the Denkyirahene, king of the Denkyira people, to an Asante leader in the late 1600s. At that time, prior to the emergence of the Asante as the major regional power, Denkyira was the largest Akan kingdom. The basin arrived with an order that the Asante were to fill it with gold dust and return it. Refusing, the Asante fought a series of wars with Denkyira, eventually defeating them in 1702 and securing their dominance in the region. Like the Armitage ewer, this metal vessel has been appropriated as a powerful symbol of Asante cultural history. Yet, imported brass basins such as this were circulating widely in the Gold Coast from at least the 1700s, and probably from much earlier. Among the Akan they were highly valued trade goods, with some incorporated into elite and royal households and passed down through the generations as prestigious heirlooms. Others were maintained by designated custodians within communities, palaces or shrines.

Measuring around a metre in diameter, the Bobrapa Pan is a type of large copper-alloy basin called a 'Neptune', brought to the West African coast by Portuguese, Dutch and British traders from the late 1400s onwards (fig. 24). A similar example, called Aya Dasuo (symbol of endurance), possibly dated to the 1500s, can be found at Manso. Pieter de Marees, a Dutch trader and explorer who travelled to what was then known in Europe as the Guinea Coast, published an account of his African journey in 1602. He included an image of a West African trader among the many engravings in his book (fig. 25). This individual, called Batafou, is shown carrying a copper plate or basin in his hand. While Neptunes appear in various documentary sources, they are rarely present archaeologically. However, a Neptune in the

24 The Bobrapa Pan, also called the Denkyira Basin, 1500–1700 (?). Germany or the Netherlands (?). Copper alloy. Diam. 100 cm. Photograph by Raymond Silverman, February 1980.

Museum für Hamburgische Geschichte, Germany – part of a late 1500s shipwreck off the coast of Wittenbergen – was probably headed for West Africa, where it was destined to be sold or exchanged as a gift (fig. 26). Other metal items from this same shipwreck include unworked copper bars or plates stamped with the trademark of the banking house responsible for the metal's extraction, Paller Augsburg.

Among the largest and most significant of all imported Neptunes is the Aya Kese (great basin), formerly located at the entrance to the Asante royal mausoleum prior to its demolition by British forces in 1896 (fig. 27). Like the Asante Ewer and the York jug, it was photographed in situ by Frederick Grant in 1884 (fig. 28). It is a vast object, measuring around 110 centimetres in diameter, and was formed from hammering a single copper ingot or sheet. The rough concentric hammer marks still visible inside the basin bear testament to this process of production. Around the rim is a series of cast elements: four resting lions with their mouths wide open and nineteen doorknob-shaped handles. Each of these is spaced relatively evenly and riveted into place, but three of the knobs are missing or were never attached. Prior to the destruction of the mausoleum, the basin was looted by Robert Baden-Powell, a senior military figure in the Fourth Anglo-Asante War. He gifted the vessel to the Royal United Services Institute, London, and it was

25 Pieter de Marees, *Beschrijvinghe ende historische verhael vant Gout Koninckrijck van Gunea (Description and historical account of the Gold Kingdom of Guinea)*, Amsterdam: Michiel Colijn, 1617, p. 16.

26 Neptune (basin), late 1500s. Southern Germany (?). Brass. H. 10.5 cm, Diam. 35 cm. Museum für Hamburgische Geschichte, 2009-2656-2.

27 Aya Kese, 1500–1700. Germany or the Netherlands (?). Copper alloy. Diam. 110 cm. National Army Museum, London, NAM. 1963-10-182-1.

28 Aya Kese outside Bantama Royal Mausoleum, 1884. Photograph by Frederick Grant. The National Archives, TNA CO 1069/31 (23).

put on display immediately in the museum at the Banqueting Hall in Whitehall Palace. Today, the basin is in the collection of the National Army Museum, London. Another, very similar vessel, however, remains in Ghana, at Abakrampa. Historian and archaeologist Gérard Chouin has documented its history, noting that it was a military trophy seized in a local war in 1868.[13] The Abakrampa vessel, therefore, aligns in community memory and shared narratives with many of the other copper-alloy vessels documented in the Gold Coast in their association with Asante military victory and successful territorial expansion, and demonstrates perhaps their key function of serving to validate or reinforce political legitimacy.

The Aya Kese is an object imbued with immense ritual and historical significance, and its fame was such that it was known about in England long before it was removed by Baden-Powell. Thomas Bowdich, who was among the earliest-known British visitors to Kumasi, in 1817, recorded his own impression of the vessel in an 1819 account:

> *The Kings, and Kings only, are buried in the cemetery at Bantama, and the sacred gold buried with them … their bones are afterwards deposited in a building there, opposite to which is the largest brass pan I ever saw, (for sacrifices,) being about five feet in diameter, with four small lions on the edge. Here human sacrifices are frequent and ordinary, to water the graves of the Kings.*[14]

Other foreign observers followed Bowdich in interpreting the Aya Kese as a basin intended for use during human sacrifices. Following the building of a new mausoleum on the site of the former royal burial ground in 1930, the Asantehene Prempeh I (1870–1931) – using the title Kumasihene (ruler of Kumasi) given to him on his return from exile by the British – wrote to colonial officials requesting the Aya Kese be returned to Bantama:

> *Now, there is only one important thing that remains … It is the 'Big Bantamah Brass Pan' … As this is a very important Vessel in the eyes of the Ashantis and it would enhance the historical character of the Mausoleum … I beg most respectfully to approach Your Honour … to recommend that the 'Pan' be returned to Ashanti.*

As part of their assessment for whether to return the basin or not, the British asked Prempeh to submit a history of the Aya Kese. In his reply, held in the Public Records and Archives Administration Department in Accra, he wrote that it pre-dated the formation of the Asante Kingdom and originally descended from heaven with a gold chain and a white stool at Asiakwa during a thunderstorm.[15] An old lady called Anchiwar Nyame also descended and eventually settled with the basin and stool at Asantemanso. On her death, her daughter succeeded her and her first male child became head of the family, establishing the matrilineal line of succession. Over time, the dispersal of different family groups created disharmony. Eventually, Oti-Aken-Ten, the grandson of Anchiwar Nyame, settled in Kumasi, bringing the brass basin with him. He was appointed king and peace reigned again. He was succeeded by Obiri Yeboa and in turn by Osei Tutu, who declared that the brass basin be installed at Bantama, the burial place of Asante kings.

Metal vessels clearly travelled great distances, from the Middle East to Africa and Europe, and from Europe to the Middle East as well as Africa. For instance, the inlaid Mamluk basin now at the Musée du Louvre, the so-called Baptistère de Saint Louis, was probably made in Damascus, Syria, between 1320 and 1340, possibly for export to Europe; its first documented appearance is in France in the 1700s, but it is likely it was there much earlier. In 1880, when the Victoria and Albert Museum acquired a group of objects associated with a reception room from Damascus, among them was a brass laver, a spouted vessel for pouring water, made in the Netherlands in the 1500s, but inscribed in Arabic with the name Hajj Lutuf al-Haytalani, probably a previous Syrian owner (fig. 29). Items like these no doubt moved through the well-oiled trade networks of the Venetian republic, which were connected throughout Europe and the Middle East. For the Asante Ewer, however, questions remain about its journey. Was it taken across the Sahara desert like the Mamluk basins surveyed by Silverman, or did it arrive on the West African coast through European maritime journeys, like the Aya Kese and other imported Neptunes? And what of the other two European jugs from the royal palace, the

York and Armitage vessels? Did they travel with the Asante Ewer from Europe to West Africa? Or are they evidence of an active system which brought a number of vessels along the same routes over a longer period? Do they share similar biographies? Unless further information comes to light, these will remain difficult questions to answer. However, by situating the Asante Ewer in the context of surviving luxury metalwork in the Akan region and the specific histories assigned to each vessel locally, it is easier to appreciate its cultural significance and potential link to Asante history. There is little to suggest that the ewer was valued because it was an English antiquity from a far-off land; it was, instead, most likely regarded as a relic of Akan history, and was possibly used to commemorate a period of Asante expansion and regional domination. That objects like the Asante Ewer served to communicate local history, ancestry and beliefs makes the looting of the royal palace following the 1895–6 Anglo-Asante War all the more shocking.

29 Laver, 1470–1500. The Netherlands. Brass. H. 28.5 cm, W. 23 cm. Victoria and Albert Museum, London, 411M-1880.

3 A military expedition and the looting of Kumasi

> *… and then the work of collecting valuables and property was proceeded with. There could be no more interesting, no more tempting work than this. To poke about in a barbarian king's palace, whose wealth has been reported very great, was enough to make it so … Here was a man with an armful of gold-hilted swords, there one with a box full of gold trinkets and rings … It need not be supposed that all the property found in the palace was of great value. There were piles of the tawdriest and commonest stuff mixed indiscriminately with quaint, old, and valuable articles, a few good brass dishes, large metal ewers …*
>
> — Robert Baden-Powell[16]

On 20 January 1896 the palace of the Asantehene Prempeh I was ransacked by British soldiers on the orders of the Governor of the Gold Coast, Sir William Edward Maxwell, following the Asantehene's enforced surrender and arrest. Robert Baden-Powell – today known as the founder of the international Boy Scouts movement – witnessed the looting of the palace and described the desecration and destruction in his subsequent publication *The Downfall of Prempeh*, a vivid account in which he details the moment that 'large metal ewers', among other things, were taken out of the king's palace. Baden-Powell served as a senior officer of the British expeditionary force assembled at Cape Coast Castle in late 1895 for the purpose of dismantling Asante authority in the region, which was perceived to be in direct conflict with British imperialist policy. This act of colonial aggression, lasting roughly from December 1895 to the end of January 1896, is often called the Fourth Anglo-Asante War or the Second Asante Expedition, which, as both these names suggest, was not an isolated episode but one in a series of violent clashes that began in the early 1800s and culminated in the annexation of the Asante state and its incorporation into the Gold Coast colony in 1902.

The confrontation of 1896, in which the medieval ewers were taken from the palace at Kumasi, has been overshadowed in cultural memory by the so-called 'Sagrenti'

Detail of fig. 30

war of 1873–4 (also known as the Third Anglo-Asante War), in which Sir Garnet Wolseley, Governor of the Gold Coast, commanded British forces against the Asante and oversaw the subsequent defeat of the Asantehene Kofi Karikari. At that time, there was widespread destruction of numerous important sites, including the Aban, the stone palace built by Asantehene Osei Bonsu in 1822. A large quantity of gold – including items of regalia, finely cast disc pendants ('soul discs') and personal ornaments – formed the official government 'spoils of war' taken in 1874. These items were brought to Britain where, having been purchased from the government by the royal goldsmiths Garrard & Co., they generated widespread interest after being put on public display. Many of these pieces were sold by Garrard's to prominent institutions such as the British Museum and the Victoria and Albert Museum, as well as to private individuals, including William Alleyne Cecil, 3rd Marquess of Exeter. The disc pendant he acquired, of impressive size, was set into a silver-gilt salver by Garrard's, its outer European form dominating the African object enclosed at its centre (fig. 30).

The purpose of this chapter, however, is to focus on the year 1896 and to review the timeline and the context for the removal of objects by British forces from Kumasi, as well as nearby Bantama. This will help to establish exactly how the three medieval ewers fit into a broader pattern of military looting. It will also frame their reception in Britain in the late 1800s and early 1900s as trophies of war.

At the outset of the 1895/6 Asante expedition, looting was officially forbidden and punishable. For example, in the 'Standing Orders for Expedition' issued to soldiers, there were reminders that: 'No village camp is to be intentionally set on fire except by order of the Colonel Commanding. Officers Commanding Corps, &c, are held responsible that no looting or unnecessary destruction of property takes place. Any infraction of this order is to be severely dealt with.'[17] Such an instruction implies that instances of (unsanctioned) looting were common and that soldiers, and affiliated personnel, needed reminding with threats of reprimand not to remove objects. When Colonel Francis Scott,

30 Silver-gilt salver 1874, London, Garrard & Co., set with gold disc pendant, Kumasi, *c.* 1850–73. Diam. 61.5 cm. British Museum, Af1973,02.1-2.

the expedition's commanding officer, first spoke with the Asantehene Prempeh I in Kumasi on 17 January, he reiterated the same official position, telling the king that 'I will be very particular and not allow any of my people to plunder … anyone caught doing so will be punished. Please understand that we will pay for everything we get'.[18]

Despite Scott's words, soldiers' diaries and documents associated with the conflict reveal that looting was nonetheless taking place. On 16 January, before British troops had even reached Kumasi, Baden-Powell noted in his diary that 'In the afternoon one of the Ansas (a royal messenger) came with a message that our levies were plundering villages. He could not give me the name of the villages.'[19] On another page, Baden-Powell recorded a note sent to a fellow senior officer, in which he stated: 'please keep your party in hand when near the town to prevent looting, and warn them against it before marching'. Furthermore, on 19 January, just two days after Scott's promise to Prempeh that he would prevent looting, Captain Thomas H. Berney of the Prince of Wales's Own Regiment of Yorkshire recorded in his diary that

> *We have been getting such curiosities as we cant. Pearce* [an officer of the regiment] *made a very lucky* [sic] *yesterday. He had to clear out a fetish house which was right in the middle of where his company is billeted and as one cannot have these fetish priests constantly about the line the edict went forth that it must be cleared. As he was doing so he came across an old bell about the size of a dinner bell with the date 1650 & and the inscription 'Amor Vincat* [sic] *Omnia' on it.*[20]

A shift in the official British position regarding looting can be pinpointed to Governor Maxwell's first interaction with Prempeh I on arrival in Kumasi following the surrender of the Asantehene and the Asantehemaa (Queen Mother) Yaa Akyaa to Colonel Scott. At this first public face-to-face with the Asantehene, on 20 January, Maxwell admonished and humiliated the king, requesting the full payment of 50,000 ounces of gold, an extraordinary amount that had been forced on the Asante as part of the Treaty of Fomena, ratified following the culmination of the 1873–4 Anglo-Asante War. Prempeh was, as might have been expected by the governor, unable to produce any such large amount of gold and was immediately arrested. There were, it seems, no plans in place about what to do with the king or with his parents and his entourage of 52 senior chiefs and confidants. He was first taken to the coast and imprisoned in Elmina Castle for nearly a year and then exiled to Sierra Leone and eventually to the Seychelles, returning to Kumasi only in November 1924 after years of pleading with colonial officials to be sent back home.

In the aftermath of the governor's decision to exile Prempeh, widespread looting was encouraged and took place across Kumasi and Bantama. On the day of Prempeh's arrest, Baden-Powell noted an order in his diary to 'Please take all immediate steps to destroy all fetish houses, groves and trees at Bantama. All money and other articles of value found are to be handed over to the camp commander.' He further described the situation when he and his soldiers entered the royal mausoleum at Bantama, a site of profound Asante ritual significance: the British troops 'Broke open back door & have about 100 prisoners. Collected all valuables – but failed to find treasure or the stool. Collected the Queen Mother's valuables.' It was then, or soon after, that Baden-Powell secured for himself the Aya Kese. Despite Scott's promise to Prempeh that he would not allow his people to plunder, and official instructions that there was to be no looting, such activity was evidently not just tolerated but encouraged. There were, however, extreme double standards. Some individuals were punished for removing objects, particularly African men local to the Gold Coast and employed to carry items for the British military, who were often the target of suspicion and prejudice. An instance of this kind of treatment is described in an anonymously written diary by a soldier in the Prince of Wales's Own Regiment of Yorkshire: 'Whilst the troops were engaged in the foregoing proceedings a number of the native carriers took advantage of the situation and commenced looting – many of them were captured in the act and will, doubtless, be severely dealt with.'[21]

As for the king's palace, which the British considered to contain the greatest riches and where the Asante Ewer was located, the governor instructed the West Yorkshire Regiment to occupy it, in an effort to make sure that all valuable items, especially those of gold and silver, were secured. The same anonymous diary relates:

> *Two Companies of the Battalion were then detailed to take charge of the Palace and prevent further looting also to secure such treasure as might be there. A large amount of gold and jewellery was taken possession of and handed over to the Governor's Staff. A sale was held later of articles of little value which were, nevertheless, curiosities, such as large umbrellas, native stools, chairs, arms, etc. These fetched very high prices.*

The looting of the palace was also recorded by Baden-Powell, referenced in the quote with which this chapter opened. Baden-Powell further describes in detail the triumphant atmosphere from a British officer's point of view inside the royal palace, clearly distinguishing between the most valuable precious-metal objects – which were 'officially'

31 'King Prempeh's Possessions Kumassi, 1896'. H. 20 cm, W. 18.3 cm. Unrecorded photographer. Prince of Wales's Own Regiment of Yorkshire Museum Charity, PH00949.1.

collected with the intention of sending them back to Britain – and 'the "loot"', which was to be sold at auction in Kumasi. However, Baden-Powell's description also demonstrates the relationship between looting, violence and destruction as a key means by which to strip away the authority as well as the cultural and spiritual identity of a conquered opponent.

Broadly speaking, three different approaches were taken to looting during the 1896 expedition. First, as documented, many objects were simply taken by soldiers, carriers and other individuals. Second, what the British determined to be high-value items, particularly those of gold and silver, were reserved for the government of the Gold Coast. These were sent back to Britain and were administered by the Colonial Office, with the vast majority later being sold, entering private collections as well as museums in Europe and the United States, where they remain today. And finally, a quantity of items – particularly those objects collected from the royal palaces and the mausoleum that were not made of precious metal, such as the Asante Ewer – were brought together and sold to soldiers and journalists at a public auction taking place over two days in Kumasi. For instance, Arthur Howell Gwynne, a Reuters journalist, recorded in his diary (now held at the Bodleian Library, Oxford) on 26 January 1896 that, on the march back to the coast, 'My chair, which forms

part of my Kumassi loot – created a gradual sensation as was dubbed all day by the villagers as Prempeh's chair.'[22]

Journalists, who potentially had more spending power than most non-commissioned military personnel, were frequently blamed by soldiers for pushing up the prices in the auction. Captain Berney of the Prince of Wales's Own Regiment of Yorkshire recalled in his diary that 'The pieces [unidentified word] things fetched were also very high the war correspondents especially bidding up to any price for the most absurd articles.' A rare surviving photograph of the auction, now badly damaged, appears to show groups inspecting items for sale (fig. 31). Although it is not possible to detail the Asante Ewer among the objects on show, it was bought at this auction by Major Charles St Leger Barter, who will be discussed in greater detail in the next chapter. The funds raised from this sale, as Maxwell reported to the Colonial Office, amounted to £150 16s 9d and were used by the governor to defray the cost of the expedition. It appears, however, that some objects were not sold at auction, nor were they deemed significant enough to be sent to Britain, but were reserved especially for Maxwell himself. Captain Berney recorded that 'The real curiosity of the loot however was retained. I believe for the governor a small piece of silver plate with the arms of Henri IV of France on it.'

What Maxwell chose to do with the majority of 'his' items is mostly unrecorded, except in certain cases – for instance, it was from the governor that the Prince of Wales's Own Regiment of Yorkshire received one of their most esteemed trophies, the other medieval jug that appears alongside the Asante Ewer in Frederick Grant's courtyard photograph. A small metal plaque in the shape of a shield located beneath its spout notes this aspect of its history, stating 'Bronze urn presented to the officers 2nd Batt P.W.O. (West Yorks Regt) at Kumassi, 17th Jan 1896 by the Governor of the Gold Coast' (fig. 32). Maxwell must have been pleased with the actions of the regiment. They not only secured the palace following Prempeh's arrest but also provided a military escort to the coast for the king's imprisonment at Elmina. Items used by Prempeh during this journey, such as his bed and chair (or, at least, items purported to be such), remain in the collection

32 Detail of shield on the York jug (see fig. 21).

33 'Asante War Trophies', 1896. R. Miller Studio, Dover. H. 18 cm, W. 20 cm. Prince of Wales's Own Regiment of Yorkshire Museum Charity, PH00945.

of the Prince of Wales's Own Regiment of Yorkshire. After being shipped back to Britain by the international transport agents Henry Hart & Co., Ltd, and arriving in Dover, these items were photographed locally by A.J. Grossman and R. Miller. In one of Miller's arrangements, the medieval ewer appears as a war trophy alongside drums, swords, stools and carefully arranged human remains (fig. 33). Local newspaper reports detail that a similar display was mounted in the window of the shipping agent Hart & Co., potentially the first exhibition of looted items from the 1896 confrontation.[23] When these objects were later transferred to the regimental mess hall, they were rearranged again, displayed proudly as a reminder of the regiment's involvement in a successful colonial campaign.

If, like Armitage's jug, the York and Asante ewers were seized as trophies during Asante military expansion, then, potentially, Frederick Grant's photograph of 1884 and Miller's picture of 1896 present an inversion of such events – from a ritual context in the royal courtyard, captured by Grant with the ewers and the sacred trees at the centre, to a grotesque and sensational one in Miller's studio, where war trophies are arranged to create a distinct image of excess and savagery. When the ewers were removed from the courtyard by the British military, their ritual significance was deactivated and replaced with a new narrative – in the case of the York jug as a spoil of war in the regimental mess, and for the Asante Ewer as a rare surviving English medieval vessel displayed at the British Museum.

4 Acquisition

> *Events have succeeded each other with such rapidity of late in West Africa that to refer to the taking of Kumassi and the possessions of King Prempeh sounds somewhat like ancient history. The greater part of the spoils obtained at the last sacking of the Ashanti capital had, however, but little interest to the Society. So far as I know, there was only this one thing from the last campaign that is of interest to us here, and I was fortunate enough to secure it from the officer to whom it fell. He had the perspicacity to prefer the 'old jug' to the ordinary savage weapons and blood-stained sacrificial stools …*
>
> — Charles Hercules Read[24]

On 10 May 1896 Major Charles St Leger Barter, 'late 2nd in Command "Special Service Corps" in Ashanti', sat down at his desk in the barracks in Pontefract, West Yorkshire, to write to British Museum curator Charles Hercules Read (fig. 34). Major Barter, who was also the Commanding Officer of the Yorkshire Light Infantry, had recently returned from West Africa where he had served in the 1895–6 Anglo-Asante War (fig. 35). Although the two men had never met, Barter was seeking Read's expert opinion on an object he had brought back with him to England. In his letter, Barter asks Read if he

> *would be so kind as to give me your opinion regarding an old English jug which was found in the Kings' palace at Kumassi. It was amongst the articles offered for sale at public auction, and I was lucky enough to secure it. The jug is in my humble opinion, of some value.*

Barter goes on to describe the Asante Ewer's weight and its metal 'of a non-rusting character', and includes a small drawing of the item, apologising for its crudeness (fig. 36). He indicates the presence of animals on the lid and in the medallions and correctly identifies the arms of England on the front, under the spout, 'with fleur-de-lys and leopard-like lions'. Furthermore, Barter offers his own interpretation of some of the 'old English characters' around the bowl of the jug, although he acknowledges that 'the English on the others is too old for me'. As for how the old 'English' vessel

34 Charles Hercules Read, 1896. Photograph by unrecorded photographer. British Museum Archive, Department of British and Medieval Antiquities and Ethnography.

35 Charles St Leger Barter, date unknown. Photograph by unrecorded photographer. King's Own Yorkshire Light Infantry Regimental Museum, Heritage Doncaster.

arrived in West Africa, Barter fancifully states: 'I cannot offer any speculation as to how the jug got to Kumassi, beyond the surmise that it may have been taken by the Crusaders to Palestine & from there worked its way through Africa, after capture by the Saracens.' Clearly impressed by the state of the jug, he indicates that only the lid is 'worse for wear', while the 'remaining figures & parts in relief are wonderfully well preserved, owing no doubt to the quality of the metal & the large quantity of mud in which it seems to have been incrusted for ages'. Barter ends the letter by asking for Read's judgement on the item's 'genuineness & age', for which he 'shall be very grateful indeed', and suggests that he could bring it to the British Museum as it was currently in London, 'lying at the United Service Club, Pall Mall'.[25]

Intrigued by the offer, Read replied to Barter two days later: 'I should be glad to see your jug: it is certainly a curiosity but scarcely so old as the Crusades, I fancy.' He encouraged him to bring the item himself or 'send the jug in advance', and Barter duly visited Read in Bloomsbury two weeks later on 30 May to deposit the object in the department of British and Medieval Antiquities and Ethnography.[26] After his visit, Barter eagerly followed up with another letter to Read on 11 June, this time addressed from Pall Mall, where he was staying at his club. He confirms that he left the jug at the Museum, and that it was 'just in the state it was in when I got it at Kumassi'. Read's prompt reply two days later reveals further details of their exchange, particularly that the two men had discussed the possibility of the British Museum acquiring the jug and what a fair price should be: 'In accordance with my promise,' Read states, 'I asked several knowing people what should be the asking price of your bronze jug. Two of them, Sir John Evans and one of the principal London dealers, said £40 (forty) and offered for sale at public auction, and I was lucky enough to secure it. The jug is in my humble opinion, of some value.

It weighs with the lid, which was attached by strong wire to the handle, about 60 lbs, and is of some dark metal of a non-rusting character. In shape it is something like the following rough sketch, for the inartistic character of which I must apologize.

It stands about 22 inches high without the lid. On this lid are animals in relief, a stag &c, but these are somewhat vague. The neck of the jug is ornamented with medalions, on each of which is represented a bird. In front are the arms of England, with fleur-de-lys

36 Extract from a letter from Charles St Leger Barter to Charles Hercules Read with drawing of the Asante Ewer, 10 May 1896. British Museum Archive, Department of British and Medieval Antiquities and Ethnography, Correspondence In, 1896, Barter, Charles St Leger.

a second dealer said £25.' At their meeting, Read might also have broached the price of comparative items, suggesting in his letter that 'the one at S[outh] Kensington', by which he meant the Robinson Jug (see page 17), 'was bought in a collection … but I have written to the owner of the collection to ask if he remembered what he gave for it'. Read ends his letter asking Barter to let him know 'how the prices I have given above strike you'.

It did not take Barter long to reply and, while he remained courteous in tone, his frustration with what he deemed a low valuation is clear. It is worth recalling here that the total realised from the two-day auction held in Kumasi was, as reported by Governor Maxwell, just over £150. Even if Barter had been willing to accept the lower valuation of £25, he would certainly have made a substantial profit in his sale of the vessel to the Museum. Barter lamented that he *must confess that the estimates regarding the value of my jug … were very disappointing to me. As I told you the other day, … I would much rather that it remained in the British Museum than anywhere else, but I have hopes that I may get better offers elsewhere, though I consider it highly probable that Sir John Evans & the other connoisseurs were quite correct in their valuation. I have been advised to have the article photographed & send copies to Berlin & Paris, & perhaps Lord Ferdinand Rothschild, with whom I am slightly acquainted.*

Read might well have been expecting such a reaction from Barter and, given his experience in haggling with hard-nosed dealers, he didn't mince his words when replying:

I am sorry but not surprised that the estimates of the value of your jug are disappointing to you. I rather inferred from what you said that your idea of its value was much greater than mine. I rather doubt whether any foreign collector or museum would care about the jug … Baron Ferdinand certainly would not care for it. I should have been ready to go a little beyond Sir John Evans' estimate but I fear you expect something a good deal higher.

Still waiting for a reply from Barter and holding out to secure the vessel for a lower price, Read nonetheless prepared an acquisition report for the Museum trustees, dated 6 July 1896. In it he asks them to approve the purchase of the jug 'at a price not exceeding £50'. He also supplied the following information:

This interesting jug has the curious history that it formed part of the loot at Kumassi. A similar one is at S. Kensington; but there is a good series in the Museum, to which the present example might be added, with great advantage. The owner has at present a very exaggerated idea of its value.[27]

Having not heard from Barter, and keen to bring the matter to a close, Read wrote to him again on 10 July to ask: 'Have you decided anything about your bronze jug?' In the same letter, Read confirmed that a dealer called Mr Harding – possibly George Harding, with whom the

Museum frequently interacted – 'came to see the jug on your behalf and may have helped you in figuring a price'.

To this, Barter excitedly replied on 14 July, stating that he

> *had a line at the same time from Baron F. de Rothschild, who thinks I would do better if I be not in a hurry to sell the jug, to wait a bit. But I would rather you had it than any other people, if we can come to an arrangement. In one of your notes you suggested that the museum authorities would be prepared to go a little further than your first suggestion. Well, if they will make the price that little more, I shall be glad to let you have the jug – at £60.*

Around the same time, Read also received a note from Ferdinand Rothschild in which the vessel makes a minor passing appearance: 'I do not know what Major Barter will do with regards to his jug but I rather think he will prefer keeping it than disposing of it for £50.' Read must have found Rothschild's interference infuriating and somewhat confusing; besides serving as a British Museum trustee, Ferdinand Rothschild had committed to donating his own significant collection from Waddesdon Manor to the Museum after his death. And so, somewhat at the end of his tether with Barter, Read replied on 15 July with his final terms. He made it clear that he still believed the original estimates to have been correct, and that he had recommended the purchase to the board of trustees at no more than £50: 'I am therefore in a position to buy the jug at once for £50, i.e. £10 more than the highest estimate of its value but I cannot buy it for £60 without further delay, and to [unidentified word] again to the Trustees. Which would you prefer?'

Several days later, on 21 July, while awaiting a final reply from Barter, Read prepared a new report for the Trustees. In it he asked them to increase the price of their offer above the £50 limit agreed previously:

> *Mr Read has the honour to report that he has now heard from Major Barter, who agrees to accept £60 for his English bronze jug. He states that he has been advised by a friend that he would get a much better price than this by waiting, but he is anxious that the jug should*

be in the Museum. Mr Read … thinks it better to give ten pounds more rather than lose the jug, which is an object of great interest to the Museum.[28]

And yet, at the time of putting together the new report for the trustees, Read had not had the final word from Barter and was evidently hedging his bets. Barter's clearly stated commitment of selling to the Museum, and his suggestion of £60 for the jug in his last letter, meant it was likely that Read was going to be able to seal the deal.

On 27 July Barter eventually replied, this time accepting the lower offer: 'As I would prefer you to have the jug than any other people, I shall accept your offer of £50. May I ask you to be kind enough to send the Arab cloth in which it was wrapped to the United Service Club.' With that, following payment to Barter, the jug was acquired by the

37 Asante drum, c. 1800–95. Made in Asante region. Wood and animal skin. H. 53 cm, W. 32 cm. King's Own Yorkshire Light Infantry Regimental Museum, Heritage Doncaster, DONRM: 456.

38 Asante stool, c. 1800–98. Made in Asante region. Wood and silver. H. 38 cm, W. 55 cm. British Museum, Af1896,0324.1.

British Museum and given the accession number 1896,0727.1. With his characteristically elegant hand, Read entered a short descriptive summary of the object into the register of acquisitions and, as was then the case with most new purchases or donations, a beautifully observed pen and ink drawing was added alongside the text. To the right-hand side of the register, in the column headed 'Observations', Read wrote: 'Obtained in the loot at Kumassi.'[29]

The Asante Ewer has routinely been treated in isolation, a single purchase from a soldier from whom the Museum acquired just one object, an extraordinary item with an even more extraordinary provenance. This is certainly how Read himself framed the item in 1898, when he presented it to the Society of Antiquaries, describing the jug as the 'one thing from the last campaign that is of interest to us here'. Barter also brought home a drum from Kumasi which, rather than offering it to the Museum, he donated to the King's Own Regiment, Lancaster (fig. 37). Whether he acquired other items at the Kumasi auction is unknown, but diaries written by soldiers on the campaign detail that the Special Service

Corps, of which Barter was Second in Command, were especially interested in acquiring loot. As for the Asante Ewer, it was certainly not Read's first acquisition from the 1896 campaign, and it would not be his last. In the months following the expedition, Read had steadily been acquiring a range of items from Kumasi. As early as 24 March, just two months after the sacking of the palace, he purchased an 'Ashanti' stool from F.R. Morton, who served in the 2nd Battalion Rifle Brigade (one of the advance Special Service Corps) (fig. 38). According to the Museum's registration slip, the stool was 'Obtained by the vendor in Prempeh's Palace Ashanti Expedition 1896'. This description does not necessarily confirm the stool came from the palace, as such a provenance, whether real or imagined, would have bolstered its desirability. On 11 May, just one day after Barter's initial letter, Read accepted seven ancestral stools and a bell from Sir William Maxwell, Governor of the Gold Coast, donated

39 'Prempeh's crown', c. 1800–95. Made in Asante region. Duiker (antelope) skin, gold and silver. H. 24 cm, W. 56 cm. British Museum, Af1900,0427.1.

via the Colonial Office. That same month, on 19 May, a military surgeon called William Owen Wolseley donated a drum, banner and sword to the Museum.

The Museum also benefited directly from its close links with the Colonial Office. On 12 May the Government of the Gold Coast donated hundreds of glass beads as well as paper amulets and gold-weights to the Museum, all of which were part of the official loot collected from Prempeh's palace. These objects arrived in Britain in three sealed boxes along with a vast quantity of gold items, but the beads were deemed unworthy for the government to keep and so were passed on to the Museum. The majority of the gold items, which travelled with the beads and comprised sword ornaments, jewellery and even a cap dubbed 'Prempeh's crown' by the press, were put on public display, first in the Royal United Services Institute and then in the Imperial Institute, before all the items were removed in late 1899 and offered to the British Museum for purchase (fig. 39). Again, Read led on the acquisition, selecting whichever items he thought appropriate and helping to facilitate the sale of the rest on behalf of the government. It is unclear when or how the majority of these 'ethnographic' objects were displayed, if at all in the period immediately after their purchase. And despite the cultural context in which the Asante Ewer was found in the Gold Coast, it immediately went on display in the gallery of medieval antiquities, where it remains today, among objects of its 'type', with little of the complex story of its African history featuring in the gallery's wider narrative.

EVERY

Epilogue

On 7 February 1961 noted anti-colonialist, socialist and provocateur Tom Driberg, Labour Member of Parliament for Barking, wrote to his fellow MP Duncan Sandys, Secretary of State for the Colonies, advocating for the return of the Asante Ewer to West Africa:

> *During a recent stay in Accra I visited the Ghana Museum … Two gaps in the collection were, however, noticeable: 1. The Museum has only a replica of an important 14th-century bronze jug which was removed from Kumasi in 1896. The original is in the British Museum … Would the B.M. let the bronze jug go (perhaps accepting the replica in exchange)?*[30]

The National Museum of Ghana, where Driberg had seen the replica, was opened on 5 March 1957, the day before Ghana gained independence from Britain. As a product of British colonialist heritage policy and that of an emerging nation-state, the collection was not simply made up of West African objects but, like the British Museum, included items from across the world, such as Roman, Greek and Egyptian antiquities, many of which were acquired as 'duplicates' from various British museums. Casts were also sought for objects identified as uniquely important, and many of these were bought directly from the British Museum. This explains the presence of the Asante Ewer, which still survives in the National Museum, remarkable for its verisimilitude (fig. 40). Its entry in the 1955 acquisition register states: 'from original in British Museum of bronze jug of Richard II of England: taken from Asantehene's Palace Kumasi in 1896'.[31] How exactly the replica was displayed remains unclear, but it is nonetheless tempting to associate its international journey and story, revealing the extent of West Africa's rich historical connections, with that of Ghanaian president Kwame Nkrumah's bold strategic vision for a newly independent, globally orientated and powerful twentieth-century country. The return of the ewer was debated further within the British government, although the documentation was

40 Cast of the Asante Ewer, c. 1955. Plaster. H. 62 cm. Ghana Museums and Monuments Board, GNM, 1955-767.

never passed on to the British Museum, so it remained unaware of any discussions. Further correspondence between colonial officials T.W. Keeble and V.E. Davies demonstrates how Driberg's suggestion was received, noting the feelings of British archaeologist/anthropologist Herbert Dennis Collings, who was curator of the National Museum of Ghana:

> *I have had a word with the Curator about the gaps Mr. Driberg noticed. Collings was horrified at any suggestion that the British Museum should surrender the 14th Century Bronze Jug. This was, in fact, a European manufactured jug made, I believe, for Richard II. Goodness knows (Mr Collings doesn't) how it ever got to Ashanti, but he is firmly of the view that it would be wrong to ask for its return and he feels that the replica they have is entirely adequate.*

Driberg received an answer on 2 June 1961 in a letter from Bernard Braine, Undersecretary of State:

> *I have now had the views of our High Commissioner in Accra on your proposals … He has reported that the 14th century bronze jug in the British Museum is in fact of European manufacture, and that, as its known historical connections are with this country rather than with Ghana it would be wrong to ask for its surrender.*

In the case of this interaction, the jug's place of production trumped its African provenance, at least in determining, according to the British Colonial Office, to which country the story of the Asante Ewer truly belonged. It is unsurprising, too, that a fear of 'surrender' was prevalent among British officials at the dawn of a post-colonial age.

Today, questions around the restitution of Asante objects, among many others from the African Continent, feature prominently in museum and academic debates and dialogues. Increasingly, these discourses are being initiated and directed by scholars, traditional leaders and members of locally invested communities in Africa and those of African heritage in the diaspora. This shift in agency is significant and timely. One of the recurring requests is for museums internationally to audit their collections. The

British Museum is committed to making its collections publicly accessible through both its online database Collection Online and its publications, such as this book, which investigate in detail the provenance of objects.

Although bound by the terms of the British Museum Act 1963 – which does not allow the de-accessioning of objects in its care (except in specific circumstances) – in 2024 the British Museum, in collaboration with the Victoria and Albert Museum, agreed a long-term loan of fifteen items of Asante regalia to Kumasi, of which thirteen were associated with looting during the Anglo-Asante wars of 1873–4 and 1895–6. This initiative came as a direct result of the personal intervention of the Asantehene Osei Tutu II. The resulting *Homecoming* exhibition marked both the 150th anniversary of the 1874 British invasion and the centenary of the return to Kumasi of Prempeh I, and later in the year was a focal point for the Asantehene's Silver Jubilee celebrations. *Homecoming* commemorates historical adversities but also acknowledges positive steps in creating new cultural cooperations between the UK and Ghana.

The ambiguity over the 'ownership' of the Asante Ewer reveals the varying trajectories that objects often follow throughout their life histories and highlights the importance of provenance research in exploring different perspectives and interpretations to gain a deeper, more nuanced understanding. While the ewer will always remain an object produced in England, this book has revealed its many complex lives, from an extraordinary jug possibly displayed at medieval feasts to a high-status item situated within the context of the long-distance trade in luxury metalwork vessels, and from a highly regarded ritual object in the courtyard of the Asante king's palace to a looted war trophy and museum acquisition.

Notes

Some of the quotations in this publication use outdated or offensive language.

1. Pers. comm., 11 February 2025.
2. Michael Siddons, *Heraldic Badges in England and Wales*, London: Society of Antiquaries, 2009, vol. II, part I, pp. 134–47.
3. Sally Badham, John Blair and Robin Emmerson, *Specimens of Lettering on English Monumental Brasses*, London, 1976.
4. Susan La Niece and Marian Campbell, 'The Asante, Robinson and Wenlok jugs: casting technology of large medieval bronze jugs', *Historical Metallurgy*, vol. 53, no. 1 (2022), pp. 19–30.
5. Charles Hercules Read, Proceedings of the Society of Antiquaries, 1898, p. 83.
6. H.B. Walters, *Church Bells of England*, London: Oxford University Press, 1912. See also A. Bayliss, 'Validating classical multivariate models in archaeology: English medieval bellfounding as a case study', PhD thesis, University College London, Institute of Archaeology, 2006.
7. Charles Hercules Read, Proceedings of the Society of Antiquaries, 1898, p. 83.
8. Raymond Silverman, 'History, Art, and Assimilation: The Impact of Islam on Akan Material Culture', PhD thesis, University of Washington, 1983. See also Silverman 2015.
9. Sarah Guérin, 'Gold, Ivory and Copper: Materials and Arts of Trans-Saharan Trade', in Berzock 2019, pp. 175–201. See also Sarah Guérin, 'Exchange of Sacrifices: West Africa in the Medieval World of Goods, *c.* 1300', *The Medieval Globe*, special issue, 'A World within Worlds? Reassessing the "Global Turn" in Medieval Art History', vol. 3, no. 2 (2017), pp. 97–124.
10. Raymond Silverman, 'Akan Kuduo: Form and Function', in *Akan Transformations: Problems in Ghanaian Art History*, ed. Doran H. Ross and Timothy F. Garrard, Los Angeles: Museum of Cultural History, University of California, 1983, pp. 10–29.
11. British Museum Archive, Collection File: Af1933,-.2-3.
12. Pers. comm., 3 April 2025: Dr Emmanuel Osei Boakye, Head of Research, Manhyia Palace Museum, Kumasi, on current naming of this pan (also known as the Denkyira Basin) and fluctuating histories of usage and acquisition.
13. Gérard Chouin, 'Forests of Power and Memory: An Archaeology of Sacred Groves in the Eguafo Polity, Southern Ghana (*c.* 500–1900 A.D.)', PhD thesis, Syracuse University, 2009, pp. 272–83.
14. Thomas Edward Bowdich, *Mission from Cape Coast Castle to Ashantee &c.*, London: John Murray, 1819, p. 289.
15. PRAAD, ADM 11/1370, File 1986/30, No.91/Case 138/30, 17 July 1930 and 'History of the Bantama Brass Pan', No. 1B.
16. Robert Baden-Powell, *The Downfall of Prempeh*, London: Methuen & Co., 1896, p. 84.
17. The National Archives, Kew, WO 107/11, Standing Orders for Expedition, 'Standing Regulations for the Ashanti Expedition'.
18. Written account of an interview between Sir Francis Scott and Prempeh I, 17 January 1896. The National Archives, Kew, WO 32/7646.
19. Robert Baden-Powell, The Ashanti Campaign, 1895–6, scrapbook and diary

held by Ghana Armed Forces Museum, Kumasi. Subsequent references to Baden-Powell's diary are from this source.

20. Diary of Captain Thomas H. Berney. Prince of Wales's Own Regiment of Yorkshire Collection, PD00085. Subsequent references to this diary are from this source.
21. Prince of Wales's Own Regiment of Yorkshire Collection, HR00171, 'The Ashanti Expedition 1895–1896, Copy of a diary kept by an N.C.O., of 2nd BN WYR'. Subsequent references to this diary are from this source.
22. Unpublished diary of Arthur Howell Gwynne, 26 January 1896, The Bodleian Library, Oxford, MS. Gwynne dep. 28 (unpaginated).
23. *The Dover Express*, 28 February 1896.
24. Charles Hercules Read, Proceedings of the Society of Antiquaries, 1898, p. 83.
25. All correspondence between Barter, Read and Rothschild can be found by the date cited in the text in the British Museum Archive, Department of British and Medieval Antiquities and Ethnography.
26. British Museum Archive, British Antiquities Visitors Book, 30 May 1896.
27. British Museum Archive, Original Papers, 6 July 1896.
28. British Museum Archive, Original Papers, no. 2634, 21 July 1896.
29. British Museum Archive, Register of Antiquities, British and Mediaeval, vol. 7, Apr 1895–July 1898, p. 193 (1896,7-27.1).
30. Tom Driberg to Duncan Sandys, 7 February 1961, The National Archives, Kew, DO 195/60. All subsequent correspondence cited in this chapter, relating to Driberg's request for the return of the Ewer, can be found in this folder.
31. Ghana National Museum, Acquisition Register, vol. 2, p. 452 (1955-767).

Further reading

Ampene, Kwasi, and Nana Kwadwo Nyantakyi III, *Engaging Modernity: Asante in the Twenty-First Century*, Ann Arbor: University of Michigan, 2014.

Baden-Powell, R., *The Downfall of Prempeh, A Diary of Life with the Native Levy in Ashanti 1895–6*, London: Methuen & Co., 1896.

Bailey, Martin, 'Two kings, their armies and some jugs. The Ashanti ewer', *Apollo*, December 1993, pp. 387–90.

Berzock, Kathleen Bickford (ed.), *Caravans of Gold, Fragments in Time: Art, Culture, and Exchange across Medieval Saharan Africa*, Princeton: Princeton University Press, 2019.

Cherry, John, and Neil Stratford, 'The Ashanti Ewers', in Neil Stratford, (ed.) *Westminster Kings and the Medieval Palace of Westminster*, London: British Museum Occasional Paper 115, 1995, pp. 98–100.

Dupuis, Joseph, *Journal of a Residence in Ashantee*, London: Henry Colburn, 1824.

Finlay, M., 'British late medieval inscribed bronze jugs: a stylistic study', *Antique Metalware Society Journal*, vol. 4, 1996, pp. 1–10.

Guérin, Sarah, 'Gold, Ivory, and Copper: Materials and Arts of Trans-Saharan Trade', in Berzock 2019, pp. 175–201.

Guérin, Sarah, 'Exchange of Sacrifices: West Africa in the Medieval World of Goods', *The Medieval Globe*, vol. 3, no. 2, 2017, pp. 97–124.

Herbert, Eugenia W., *Red Gold of Africa: Copper in Precolonial History*, Madison: The University of Wisconsin Press, 1984.

Kumler, Aden, 'Lyric Vessels', in C.M. Cervone and N. Watson (eds), *What Kind of a Thing is a Middle English Lyric?*, Philadelphia: University of Pennsylvania Press, 2022, pp. 182–217.

Kyerematen, Alexander, *Guide to Ghana Cultural Centre, Kumasi*, 1970.

Lovelace, Antonia, 'War Booty: Changing Contexts, Changing Displays: Asante "Relics" from Kumasi, Acquired by the Prince of Wales's Own Regiment of Yorkshire in 1896', *Journal of Museum Ethnography*, no. 12, 2000, pp. 147–60.

La Niece, Susan, and Marian Campbell, 'The Asante, Robinson and Wenlock jugs: casting technology of large medieval bronze jugs', *Historical Metallurgy*, vol. 53, no. 1, 2019, pp. 19–30.

McCaskie, Tom, *Asante, Kingdom of Gold: Essays in the History of an African Culture*, Durham: Carolina Academic Press, 2015.

McLeod, Malcolm D., 'Richard II, Part 3, at Kumase', in David Henige and Tom McCaskie (eds), *West African Economic and Social History: Studies in Memory of Marion Johnson*, Madison: African Studies Program at the University of Wisconsin, 1990, pp. 171–4.

McLeod, M.D., *The Asante*, London: British Museum Publications, 1981.

Prempeh I, Otumfuo, Nana Agyeman, *'The History of Ashanti Kings and the whole country itself' and Other Writings*, Oxford: Oxford University Press, 2003.

Read, Charles, *Proceedings of the Society of Antiquaries*, Second Series, vol. XVII, London, 1898.

Schulz, Vera-Simone, 'Artistic Exchanges Across Afro-Eurasia. A Global Taste for Metal Artifacts from Mamluk Syria and Egypt in Italy, West Africa, and China in the Fourteenth and Fifteenth Centuries', *Convivium*, vol. 7, no. 2, 2020, pp. 132–57.

Silverman, Raymond, 'Material Biographies', *History in Africa*, vol. 42, 2015, pp. 375–95.

Silverman, Raymond, 'Red Gold: Things Made of Copper, Brass and Bronze', in Berzock 2019, pp. 256–67.

Vale, Malcolm, 'From the Court of Richard II to the Court of Prempeh I: The problem of the "Asante" ewers', in P. Coss and C. Tyerman (eds), *Soldiers, Nobles and Gentlemen: Essays in Honour of Maurice Keen*, Cambridge: Boydell & Brewer, 2009, pp. 335–54.

Wilks, Ivor, *Asante in the Nineteenth Century: The Structure and Evolution of a Political Order*, Cambridge: Cambridge University Press, 1989 (rev. ed.).

Acknowledgements

First and foremost, grateful thanks are due to the British Academy and the Wolfson Foundation for generously funding the research that underpins this book. Our sincere thanks to Nicholas and Jane Ferguson, as well as to Sam Fogg, for supporting the production of this volume. We are immensely grateful to you.

Thanks to the hardworking staff of archives, libraries and museums across Britain that we have called upon during the writing of this book, particularly Elizabeth Haines at The National Archives, Kew, our colleagues at the York Army Museum – Eleanor Davison, Allison Freeman, Graeme Green and Caroline Pheby – and Adam Jaffer of Leeds City Museum.

In Ghana, we have been grateful for generous assistance from colleagues at the Ghana National Museum, particularly Elizabeth Asafo-Adjei, Naa Bulley and Malik Saako Mahmoud. Thanks also to staff at the Public Records and Archives Administration Department in Accra and Kumasi, with special thanks to Millicent Aryee, and to those at the Manhyia Palace Museum Archives. Staff and colleagues at the Manhyia Palace Museum and the Ghana Armed Forces Museum, Kumasi, also kindly supported the research in Ghana; special thanks are due to Emmanuel Osei Boakye, Justice Brobbey, Abdulai Seidu, Gordon Frimpong and Emmanuel Quainoo. Thanks also to the Very Reverend Daniel French of the Wesleyan Methodist Church in Accra.

A group of experts generously read through the text, saving us from many errors, although those that remain are ours alone. Thanks to: Gilbert Amegatcher, John Cherry, Jill Cook, Sarah Guérin, Malcolm McLeod, Sam Nixon, Ray Silverman and Daniel Wakelin. Additional thanks to Ray for kindly allowing us to reproduce his images.

Special thanks to Michael Neilson at the British Museum and colleagues from the Crucible Foundry: Sam Dalton, Matt Borthwick and Ermanno Elia, as well as Tim Demier from Arts Heritage for sharing their knowledge and time in exploring the production techniques for medieval ewers with us.

At the British Museum, particular thanks to Director Nicholas Cullinan and Director of Public Engagement Jill Maggs for supporting this and related projects. Thanks also to David Agar, Helen Anderson, Tunde Babalola, James Baker, Sarah Blencowe, Hayley Browne, Hugo Chapman, Emily Collins-Owen, Zoe Cormack, James Dear, Ruby Eyre, Julia Farley, Joanna Fernandes, Vikki Hawkins, Jim Hamill, Jill Hasell, Thomas Heal, Carl Heron, JD Hill, Rachel King, Xerxes Mazda, Cynthia McGowan, Aude Mongiatti, Anne Nielsen, Laura Peruchetti, Jim Peters, Maryam Philpot, Eleanor Schelpe, Isabel Seligman, Naomi Speakman, Melanie Waha, Richard Wakeman, Stewart Watson and Megan Wilcock. We would particularly like to thank Lydia Cooper for her exceptional work in bringing this publication to fruition, and the rest of the Publishing team – Claudia Bloch, Beata Kibil, Laura Meachem and Toni Allum – as well as designer Adrian Hunt, copyeditor Robert Sargant and proofreader Phoebe Colley.

Thanks also to Sophia Adams, Martin Bailey, Jessica Barker, Nicholas Badcott, Paul Basu, Alixe Bovey, Marian Campbell, Gerard Choin, Philippe Cordez, Terri Dendy, Christopher Dobbs, Sonja Drimmer, Tristram Hunt,

Aden Kumler, Yona Lesger, Mary-Ann Middlekoop, Tom Nickson, William Nsuiban Gmayi, Chris Gosden, Michael Graham-Stewart, Sandy Heslop, Julian Luxford, Angus Patterson, Barnaby Phillips, Chris Pickford, Liz Robertson, James Robinson, Lynsey Slater, Abubakar Sule, Kristen Windmuller-Luna, Chris Wingfield and Michaela Zöschg.

Finally, thanks to our friends and families, especially Peter, Esther, Adelaide and Isaac.

Credits

The publisher would like to thank the copyright holders for granting permission to reproduce the images illustrated. Every attempt has been made to trace accurate ownership of copyrighted material in this book. Any errors or omissions will be corrected in subsequent editions provided notification is sent to the publisher.

Further information about the Museum and its collection can be found at britishmuseum.org. Registration numbers for British Museum objects are included in the image captions. Unless otherwise stated, copyright in photographs belongs to the institution mentioned in the caption. All images of British Museum objects are © 2025 The Trustees of the British Museum, courtesy the Department of Photography and Imaging.

Figs 1, 28, pp. 66–7: The National Archives, ref. CO 1069/31 (17), ref. CO 1069/31 (23)
Figs 3, 17: © Bibliothèque nationale de France
Figs 7, 8: © The National Gallery, London. All rights reserved
Fig. 9: Courtesy the Victoria and Albert Museum, London and The Culture Trust, Luton. Photo © The Trustees of the British Museum
Figs 10, 29: © Victoria and Albert Museum, London
Figs 11, 14: Photographs by Adrian Kotlarz, reproduced by the kind permission of The Culture Trust, Luton
Fig. 12: Drawing by Craig Williams © The Trustees of the British Museum
Fig. 15: Map by Martin Brown © The Trustees of the British Museum
Figs 16, 24: Courtesy Raymond Silverman
Fig. 21: Courtesy of the PWO Museum Charity
Fig. 26: Courtesy of the Museum für Hamburgische Geschichte
Fig. 27: Image courtesy of the National Army Museum, London
Figs 31, 32, 33: Copyright held by the Prince of Wales's Own Regiment of Yorkshire Museum Charity
Figs 35, 37: King's Own Yorkshire Light Infantry Regimental Museum, Heritage Doncaster
Fig. 40: Courtesy Ghana Museums and Monuments Board / Photo by Lloyd de Beer